THE DEPTH OF THE SOUL

Journaling thoughts of:
THEODORE WEAVER

ISBN 979-8-88540-779-3 (paperback)
ISBN 979-8-88540-780-9 (digital)

Christian Faith Publishing
832 Park Avenue
Meadville, PA 16335
www.christianfaithpublishing.com

Printed in the United States of America

CONTENTS

CHAPTER 1

Because You Are with Me, I Am Secure

Because you are with me, I am safe and secure. "Oh God, thou art my God; early will seek thee…" First thing in the morning, I'm thinking about Him; even if I'm not on my knees, I need his guidance through the day. "…My soul thirsteth for thee in a dry and thirsty land, where no water is" (Psalm 63:1). If the star Wormwood hits the earth and causes famine and destroys the fresh water supply to a third of mankind, you'll be with me where no water is, or you'll guide me to a fresh water source (Revelation 8:10–11).

"To see thy power and thy glory, so as I have seen thee in the sanctuary" (Psalm 63:2). Every time I'm thinking of the wrong stuff (and there is a lot), I see him in the sanctuary in my soul, pointing me in the right direction. "Because thy loving-kindness is better than life, my lips shall praise thee" (Psalm 63:3). I can't imagine myself ever being without Him; it would be like not having oxygen. His power and glory are clear when we look at 2 Thessalonians 1:6–10:

> Seeing it is a righteous thing with God to recompense tribulation to them that trouble you; And to you who are troubled rest with us, when the Lord Jesus shall be revealed from heaven with His mighty angels, In flaming fire taken vengeance on them that know not God, and that obey not the gospel of our Lord Jesus Christ…

In order to not obey something, you must know what it is that you're not obeying. What about Christians that know the gospel and don't keep it?

> …Who shall be punished with everlasting destruction from the presence of the Lord, and from the Glory of His Power; When He shall come to be glorified in His Saints and to be admired in all of them that believe because our testimony among you was believed in that day.

"Thus will I bless thee while I live: I will lift up my hands in thy name" (Psalm 63:4). And I will bless thee at death as I enter into the bliss of heavenly glory. I'll be so happy my hands won't know what to do but hug every saint I can find as I move through the crowd, to hug the one that hung on the cross so that I could have eternal life, and his name is Jesus.

"My soul shall be satisfied as with marrow and fatness" (bone marrow produces two hundred billion red blood cells every day). There's power in the blood. Just think when you receive Jesus as your personnel savior, He's in you; there's life in the blood. Keep your spiritual life healthy, and your soul will be fat.

"And my mouth shall praise thee with joyful lips" (Psalm 63:5). When I hear that phrase, I just know it's the heavenly language. "When I remember thee upon my bed, and meditate on thee in the night watches" (Psalm 63:6). When I lay my head down at night, I pray and fall in sweet sleep in Jesus. "Because thou hast been my help, therefore in the shadow of thy wings will I rejoice" (Psalm 63:7).

As chicks run to get under the mother hen's feathers for protection and warmth, so do we run to thee. In Psalm 91:4, it says, "He shall cover thee with his feathers, and under his wings shalt thou trust: his truth shall be thy shield and buckler." "My soul followeth hard after thee…" I have my face as flint; even if it is a shameful thing that I might be going through, he is right there with me. He will have "…His right hand out holding me up" (Psalm 63:8). "But those that seek my soul, to destroy it, Shall go into the lower parts of the earth" (Psalm 63:9).

Satan and his angels will end up in the molten magma in the core of the earth till God sends them to the lake of fire. They shall fall by the sword; the Word of God is a two-edged sword. If they are wicked, evil humans, they shall fall by the sword, spoken of in Romans 13:4.

"And their flesh will be eaten by jackals, (foxes)" (Psalm 63:10). "But the king shall rejoice in God; every one that sweareth by Him shall glory: but the mouth of them that speak lies shall be stopped." (Psalm 63:11) The leader of any country in the free world that is a born-again believer will no doubt rejoice because that country is probably supporting Israel for they are God's chosen people. (Note: This Psalm was quoted by General George Patton during the war in Europe.)

CHAPTER 2

Healing from Above

The Lord Jesus begins by saying to a cripple, "Thy sins be forgiven thee," after which he adds, "Arise and walk." The pardon of sin and healing of sickness complete one to the other for in the eyes of God, who sees our entire nature, sin and sickness are as closely united as the body and the soul. If you're not a born-again believer, you don't know that some of the things you're doing can bring sickness and death, but if you're saved, God would direct you always from those things.

Drugs, homosexuality, alcohol, adultery, stealing, and so on will make you sick or put you in prison. Sometimes, we could eat bad food or be in a not-so-sanitary environment and get sick. When I went on a mission's trip into the Amazon rainforest in Brazil, I got sick; maybe it was the food, or maybe I didn't wash my hands before I ate.

We were in an area to baptize some of the locals, and one boy we cast a demon out of earlier in the week got baptized. I happened to be sick that very day, and the Lord spoke to me to remember the scripture for when God told Naaman to dip himself in the Jordan to be healed of leprosy. "Then went he (Naaman) down, and dipped himself seven times in Jordan, according to the saying of the man of God…" (2 Kings 5:14).

So I went down to the Amazon where the baptizing was going on and got baptized. One hour later, I was healed. This is recorded on a YouTube video by Far-Flung Tin Can ministries that recorded live in the Amazon. It's called "Joy in the Waters." In the book of James, it says as follows:

> Is any among you afflicted? Let him pray. Is any merry? Let him sing psalms. Is any sick among you? Let him call for the elders of the church; and let them pray over him, anointing him with oil in the name of the Lord: And the prayer of faith shall save the sick, and the Lord shall raise him up; and if he has committed sins, they shall be forgiven him. Confess your faults one to another, and pray one for another, that ye may be healed. The effectual fervent prayer of a righteous man availeth much. (James 5:13–16)

This is for a Christian that has fallen into sin, and this sin has caused this sickness. Christians should know that if they're in a position to pray for someone to be healed, lay hands on them, and pray that they be healed. They don't have to know Christ to be healed. In the Bible, Jesus healed many that were sick and casted out demons, and they didn't even know who he was; most of the time, Jesus was outside and not in the synagogue.

Street ministry is important. You see the Master (Jesus) was a master at street ministry. When in Africa in 2000, I was with a group from the States, looking to buy land to build an orphanage. We ran into a group of people that appeared to be in a church service of a sort. We come to find out that it was a witch doctor.

The people were responsive to the witch doctor's power. We entered the group and started pleading the blood of Jesus and rebuking this wicked spirit. The witch doctor finally left reluctantly and took his drummer with him. The people thought they were being healed and that the witch doctor was sending away evil spirits. This shows how people can be deceived by false teaching or a false prophet.

When we started praying and laying hands on the sick and unfortunate, the truth was manifested. They were falling out in the spirit left and right, and we had to be careful not to step on anyone. Remember, the dark side has prayers to their leader. The Bible says the God of this world has blinded the minds of those who believe not. When you are touched by the Spirit of the living God, whether he healed you or not, you'll know it was the anointed one.

The Bible tells us in 1 Thessalonians the following:

> Now we exhort you, brethren, warn them that are unruly, comfort the feeble-minded, support the weak, be patient toward all men. See that none render evil for evil unto any man; but ever follow that which is good, both among yourselves, and to all men. Rejoice evermore. Pray without ceasing. In everything give thanks: for this is the will of God in Christ Jesus concerning you. Quench not the Spirit. Despise not prophesyings. Prove all things; hold fast that which is good. Abstain from all appearance of evil. And the very God of peace sanctify you wholly; and I pray God your whole spirit and soul and body be preserved blameless unto the coming of our Lord Jesus Christ. (1 Thessalonians 5:14–23)

Follow these scriptures to the letter, and your health will increase.

The record of creation tells us that man is composed of three parts. God created man from the dust of the earth and breathed into him the breath of life: all of living, breathing creation even on the level of the cell structure and DNA. God spoke into existence through his Son, Jesus Christ.

In the Book of John, it says the following:

> In the beginning was the Word, and the Word was with God, and the Word was God. The same was in the beginning with God. All things were made by him; and without him was not

anything made that was made. In him was life; and the life was the light of men. (John 1:1–4)

So, my brothers and sisters, he made you, and he can heal you. The breath of God was breathed in you in the beginning of your life. When you reach the age of reason, I would pray that the building blocks of your soul would receive him as your personal savior so you'll be locked into glory. God breathed himself and his spirit into you.

By this connection of spirit with matter, the man becomes a living soul. The soul, with the mind, is who the man actually is. It finds its place between the body and the spirit; it is the link that molds them together. By the body, the soul finds itself in relation to the external world and, by the spirit, with the world invisible and with God.

With the soul, the spirit can subject the body to the action of the heavenly powers and spiritualize it; by means of the soul, the body also can act upon the spirit and attract it earthward. The soul listening to both the spirit and the body is in a position to choose between the voice of God, speaking through the spirit, and the voice of the world, speaking through the flesh. If you are a born-again believer, listen to the spirit, and live in good health.

CHAPTER 3

Life after Death

We, as Christians, wonder and/or fear about the afterlife. In the Book of John, it says the following:

> Marvel not at this for the hour is coming that all that are in the graves shall hear His voice, and shall come forth; they that have done good unto the resurrection of life; and they that have done evil, unto the resurrection of damnation. (John 5:28–29)

> Jesus said, I am the resurrection and the life: he that believeth in me though he were dead yet shall he live: and whosoever liveth and believeth in me shall never die. Believeth thou this? (John 11:25–26).

If Jesus lives in you, you will want to do good things. "The fruit of the spirit is love, joy, peace longsuffering, gentleness, goodness, faith, meekness, and temperance" (Galatians 5:22–23). These are the things that make Christians do good things. Some believe that if they are just really good, they will get to heaven. Or if they leave a lot of money to the church, they will get right in. The Bible does not say that. Jesus is the only way.

I challenge you to just read the Book of John or the first epistle of John and ask the God of the Christian Bible to reveal the truth to you in the name of the Lord Jesus Christ. When you genuinely receive Jesus into your innermost being, truth will be revealed to you. He will guide you right into his heavenly glory if you let him.

What is death? The heart stops beating, so the blood stops flowing through the body. You will no longer take a breath, and that's a scary thought if heaven is not your future. We have to know that if Jesus lives in us, we will fall asleep in sweet Jesus. If you're a born-again believer, the Bible says, "We are in heavenly places in Christ Jesus" (Ephesians 2:6).

Second Corinthians 5:8 says, "We are confident, I say, and willing rather to be absent from the body, and to be present with the Lord." This scripture tells me that if we are going to be present with the Lord, our spirit and soul will be there also.

> For we know that if our earthly house of this tabernacle were dissolved, we have a building of God, an house not made with hands, eternal in the heavens. For in this we groan, earnestly desiring to be clothed upon with our house which is from heaven: If so be that being clothed we shall not be found naked (2 Corinthians 5:1–3)

The Bible says in 1 Corinthians that the "sting of death is sin" (1 Corinthians 15:56). So stay clear of sin, and repent when you do sin for God knows we are not perfect. So does the spirit of death live in you or the spirit of life? In Roman 8, it says, "For the Law of the spirit of life in Christ Jesus hath made me free from the law of sin and death" (Romans 8:2).

The law of the spirit of life will bring life eternal in heaven. I have seen two visions of what heaven will be like. The first was when I was in the woods out behind the shop at lunchtime, praying with my eyes closed. When I opened my eyes, everything was surrounded by a golden glow. This lasted for at least ten minutes.

The next vision I had, God showed me the tree of life. It was huge and covered with fruit, and the fruit looked like eggplant but was gold in color. There were as many leaves as there were fruit. The leaves were a shade of green that I cannot identify.

The law of sin and death will bring life eternal in hell, not a hard choice for most.

> The god of this world has blinded the minds of those that believe not. Thy will suffer damnation. Lest the light of the glorious gospel of our Lord and savior, Jesus Christ comes into their heart and reveals the truth to their heart. (2 Corinthians 4:4)

Just look around you; look at a baby, what a most-perfect vision of love and purity, and this baby needs its father and mother for everything until it learns how to be responsible, to take care of itself, like Mary and Joseph did for Jesus till God the Father called him into ministry. We need *God* the Father to guide us through to adulthood to become responsible Christians.

The road to glory is sometimes rough. We have to be purged from the old self. If we walk in him, death will not be a worry (well, not really death). To the born-again believer, it is life. We will pass into another dimension, and pain will be far removed. The Bible says, "The sting of death is sin." Keep a repentant heart, and when conviction hits you, that lets you know to ask for forgiveness.

I have been told that heaven is bliss, which is extreme happiness. I personally believe we will pass into another dimension. To me, the new heaven and the new earth are here, but no sin or wrongdoing is in heaven. The Bible tells in 2 Peter, "Nevertheless, we, according to his promise, look for new heavens and a new earth, wherein dwelleth righteousness" (2 Peter 3:13).

We know that even being a Christian, sin and wrongdoing still show up and raise its ugly head, but when that day comes, when he calls us home to heaven, we will be met by bliss. In one hundred and twenty years, everyone on the earth, from this date, will be dead. If you are saved, there will be no death. Everlasting life means you will pass from one life to another.

Everyone has eternal life; it will be in heavenly glory or hell and damnation. Only through the Lord Jesus Christ will you escape hellfire. Death could be in the next second. Almighty God controls the switch of life and death. Give your life to Jesus before it's too late. Look forward to leaving this life. The next life will have "no more pain and no more sorrow for the former things will pass away" (Revelation 21:4).

I believe that all the things that we wanted to do in this life that are good and good for you, Almighty God would want us to do them. I also believe that because Solomon's temple had open flowers carved in the temple (1 Kings 6:29), heaven will be full of beautiful flowers. An open flower also represents resurrection, and yes, I love flowers.

CHAPTER 4

That Which Was from the Beginning

"That which was from the beginning…" (I John 1:1). That is a powerful statement. In other words, there was nothing before him. You could lose your mind just thinking how that could even be. The apostles heard Jesus speak as they followed him everywhere. Yes, Jesus was from the beginning. He just took a side trip into our neighborhood to speak to us through the pages of the Bible and gave himself for us on an old rugged cross.

If you want to see what they looked upon, let's see what Isaiah 53 says. We look at Jesus as someone that is full of joy and love, playing with the children, but he was carrying the sins of the world on his shoulders, and the longer he was on the earth, the heavier it got. Isaiah says the following:

> For he shall grow up before him as a tender plant, and as a root out of a dry ground: he hath no form nor comeliness; and when we shall see him, there is no beauty that we should desire him. He is despised and rejected of men; a man of sorrows, and acquainted with grief: and we hid as it were our faces from him; he was despised, and we esteemed him not. Surely he hath borne our griefs, and carried our sorrows: yet we did esteem him stricken, smitten of God, and afflicted. But

he was wounded for our transgressions, he was bruised for our iniquities: the chastisement of our peace was upon him; and with his stripes we are healed. (Isaiah 53:2–5)

Never forget, he came to destroy the works of the devil. So when evil and wrongdoing are coming against you, remember Colossians:

Who hath delivered us from the power of darkness, and hath translated us into the kingdom of his dear Son: In whom we have redemption through his blood even the forgiveness of sins. To whom God would make known what is the riches of his glory of this mystery among the gentiles; which is CHRIST IN YOU, THE HOPE OF GLORY. (Colossians 1:13–14, 27)

The devil has no place in you (stay clear of sin). John had seen what Christ went through when he wrote 1 John. It was dated between AD 85 and 90 from Ephesus, so he saw the apostles go before him. He saw and heard Jesus preach and was at the last supper and watched him get nailed to a cross and die on that cross. He saw him placed in a tomb and resurrected from the grave and ascended into Heaven. "…And our hands have handled, of the Word of life" (1 John 1:1).

Jesus said, "I am the way, the truth, and the life" (John 14:6). How are you handling the word of life and not just the name Jesus but the name of the Son of the living God (Jesus) when you receive him as your personal savior? That name will keep you healthy. That name will keep food on the table. That name will keep you out of trouble and get you out of trouble. That name will keep you from hell and damnation. Psalm 91 says the following:

Because he hath set his love upon me, therefore will I deliver him: I will set him on high, because he hath known my name. He shall call upon me, and I will answer him: I will be with him in trouble; I will deliver him, and honour him. With long life will I satisfy him, and show him my salvation. (Psalm 91:14–16)

That name of the word of life is the *Lord Jesus Christ*. For the life was manifested, the true character of God is brought forth through the Son, and we have seen it and bear witness. In other words, we have proof. "And shew unto you that eternal life, which was with the Father, and was manifested unto us" (1 John 1:2).

By this time, the apostles have seen Jesus raise the dead and resurrect from the grave and ascend into heaven. "That which we have seen and heard declare we unto you, that ye also may have fellowship with us: and truly our fellowship is with the Father, and with his Son Jesus Christ" (1 John 1:3). How can we have fellowship with the apostles and Jesus in the twenty-first century? Read and digest the Word of God. Spend time with the Word, and you'll be fellowshipping with the author and those that were inspired to write it.

"These things write we unto you, that your joy may be full" (1 John 1:4). And you know what they say: true joy comes only from heaven. "This then is the message, which we have heard of him, and declare unto you, that God is Light, and in Him is no darkness at all" (1 John 1:5).

I don't know why some Christians live a double life; maybe they are only a Christian on Sunday, or they are using the Word to fill their bank account with cash. Verse 6 says, "If we say that we have fellowship with him, and walk in darkness, we lie and do not the truth" (1 John 1:6). We have to be careful in this year of 2021.

Paganism, witchcraft, and Wicca are growing at a rapid pace, and a lot of these are proclaimed Christians. When in Brazil in 2018, the minister of the church in Brazil said that there is a lot of witchcraft in the mainline churches in South America. Check out the trips in India and the Brazilian rainforest on the Facebook of Far-Flung Tin Can.

Also, in this book, read chapter "Missions Across the World" for more details. This is a record of my travels across the globe, before and after Jesus Christ. "But if we walk in the light, as he is in the light, we have fellowship one with another and the blood of Jesus Christ his Son cleanseth us from all sin" (1 John 1:7).

His light comes from the light of the Father. Don't forget; Jesus is God on earth. We are all connected by spiritual DNA, just like a wife is hurt when her husband is hurt because of their connection. If we say that we have no sin, we haven't been born yet. You're still in the womb. If you're not born-again, you are incased in sin, so "if you say I have no sin you deceive yourself, and the truth is not in you" (1 John 1:8).

Jesus is the truth. When you receive Jesus and ask for forgiveness, truth enters the soul and will manifest the sin. "If we confess our sins, he is faithful and just to forgive us our sins, and cleanse us from all unrighteousness" (1 John 1:9). See, he is a faithful and a just God; he cannot lie, so if you repent, he has to forgive you because it is the Word.

If we say that we have not sinned, come on! I'll bet you lie about a lot of other things. We have all sinned and fallen short of the glory of God (Romans 3:23)—yes, even when you're a Christian. This is for a Christian: if you're not a born-again believer, you are in just, plain sin. If you're not putting the Word in, bad things could happen (1 John 1:10).

CHAPTER 5

The Truth Lies Within

Where does your truth lie? The Bible says, "To love God and keep his commandments are the beginning of wisdom." If our wisdom is covered by truth, it should not be hard to follow God's commandments. If you're a born-again believer, his law is written on the tables of your heart. If you're a Christian, which dabbles with sin, you might need the Ten Commandments to wake you up to the truth. In 1 Corinthians, it says the following:

> Know ye not that the unrighteous shall not inherit the kingdom of God? Be not deceived: neither fornicators, nor idolaters, nor adulterers, nor effeminate, nor abusers of themselves with mankind. Nor thieves, nor covetous, nor drunkards, nor revilers, nor extortioners, shall inherit the kingdom of God. And such were some of you: but ye are washed, but ye are sanctified, but ye are justified in the name of the Lord Jesus, and by the spirit of our God. (1 Corinthians 6:9–11)

So why are you still doing those things? Are you not worried about your inheritance? What is your heart telling you when you're tempted to do things that are against the Ten Commandments? Yes, you might say, "The Ten Commandments are the old law," but my brothers and sisters, it is still the law. The book of Romans says, "The law of the spirit of life in Christ Jesus has set me free from the law of sin and death" (Romans 8:2).

Jesus Christ breaks the hold of death when you receive him; then the law is planted in your heart, so you won't have to carry stone tablets around to keep you straight. Otherwise, you'll be carrying a stone tablet that says RIP on the way to hell. The pure truth is, Jesus was born of a virgin, turned water into wine, raised Lazarus from the dead, cast out demons, told the devil to go fly a kite, healed a soldier's ear, died on a cross at Calvary, rose from the dead as seen by over five hundred people, and ascended into heaven, all for our sins and to ensure that we would have eternal life if we would receive him.

Now, that is truth, and I'll be living proof of it because I'm planning on going to heaven. The Bible says, "The truth will set you free." So the truth will come, when you're transformed by the renewing of your mind, by reading and digesting the word of God. Jesus said, "I am the way, the truth, and the life." When Jesus comes into your life, you will start to have purpose. Knowledge will increase in your life, but pray seriously for wisdom (divine wisdom), and your life will be prosperous in the good things in life.

The secret religions have a lot of knowledge, but they took of the forbidden fruit of the tree of the knowledge of good and evil, and their mind is seared with a hot iron. Only the blood of the Lamb will set them free. Their God is Lucifer, and he has blinded the minds of those that believe not.

A newborn baby is pure. God allowed this innocent creation to come into this earth through the womb of a human being; when it is born, it is born into sin. The baby might have been conceived in sin, but it is still connected to heaven. When a baby is aborted, he takes it back into his loving arms to heaven. God is waiting patiently for them to repent for what they had just done because he wants the mother to be reunited with her little wonder.

Just like the earth before it was formed on the sixth day, everything was in that mass—animals ready to come forth, seeds ready to sprout, birds standing by for flight, and fish ready to swim. With a baby, everything is in that baby; everything that baby will do is already in that baby. It will be the chaos of life that will bring it forth. That is truth. Psalm 139 states the following:

> For thou hast possessed my reins: thou hast covered me in my mother's womb. I will praise thee; for I am fearfully and wonderfully made: marvelous are thy works; and that my soul knoweth right well. My substance was not hid from thee, when I was made in secret, and curiously wrought (to variegate or the DNA) in the lowest parts of the earth. Thine eyes did see my substance, yet being imperfect; and in thy book all my members were written, which in continuance were fashioned, when as yet there was none of them. (Psalm 139:13–16)

CHAPTER 6

God Is and Always Will Be

God is and always will be. How can that be? Where was he before time was? I believe that he was, or we would not be here. Because his Son died on the cross, I am on my way to eternity in heaven, but how can that be? Why did he create me and all that is around me? I will spend days trying to figure out this incredible God. Before I was saved, I was trying to figure out who or what started all this and why (Father, show me the mystery of your glory). The Bible says, in the book of John, the following:

> In the beginning was the Word, the Word was with God, and the Word was God. The same was in the beginning with God. All things were made by him; and without him was not anything made that was made. In him was life; and the life was the light of men. And the light shineth in darkness; and the darkness comprehended it not. (John 1:1–5)

In this scripture, is darkness Satan? It sounds like it's a person or a being or maybe an inner-dimensional being. In the book of Hebrews, it talks about the express image of God.

> Who being the brightness of His glory, and
> express image of His person, and upholding all
> things by the Word of His power when He had
> by Himself purged our sins, sat down on the right
> hand of the Majesty on High. (Hebrews 1:3)

During World War II, we dropped an atomic bomb on Japan. It was so bright and hot; it put the image of a person on a rock wall as they walked by. If God was walking by that same wall during that blast, the image on the wall would look like Jesus Christ. God is God, but he used his Son, Jesus Christ, who is the Word that became flesh and dwelled among us, to create all that is.

Satan, since he has been around for thousands of years and before creation, does not have the power of creation but has the power to manipulate creation by dabbling with the genome and splicing into the DNA strand, then adding the spirit of darkness to the mix, not to mention fallen-angel DNA mixed with human women to produce a hybrid creation (Genesis 6:1–4) that God had to destroy with the flood.

Since you cannot kill a spirit even till this day, we are dealing with the demons that the flood left behind. So the first two chapters of the book of Genesis talk about creation. The third chapter busts it all up because the serpent showed up; now, we do not really know what the serpent looked like. We do know that Satan is a shape-shifter and that he has an army of fallen angels to do his dirty work, but God also told the serpent, "Upon thy belly shalt thou go, and dust shalt thou eat all the days of thy life."

Now, we know that Satan is an inner-dimensional being, so he does not require the food of the earth as we do; although if he looked like a human, he would probably eat the food of the earth, so we would think he was one of the guys, but I think when God said he would eat dust all the days of his life, it is because he is a created being and not a God and confined to the earth and not heaven. In the book of Isaiah, it says the following:

> Yet thou shalt be brought down to hell, to
> the sides of the pit. They that see thee shall nar-
> rowly look upon thee, and consider thee, saying,
> Is this the man that made the earth to tremble,
> that did shake kingdoms. (Isaiah 14:15–16)

Satan uses earthly rulers to do his bidding, and Satan only has power if we give it to him. He has a bow but no arrows (Revelation 6:2). He tries to shoot spiritual arrows at us, but the shield of faith will put those flaming arrows out in the name of Jesus Christ. What is it with the cross? When you're a Christian, you know that Christ died on that old rugged cross for our sins. He died as us. "There is no greater love, than when one lays down their life for a brother" (John 15–13). And let us not forget, he also died on the cross to destroy the works of the devil.

When I was baptized in a farm pond, the devil was under my feet as I stepped into the water. Baptism is more powerful than some think. When I was in the Brazilian rainforest in October 2018, I was very sick. The *Lord* told me to get baptized in the Amazon River. An hour later, I was healed. The Bible says, "Submit yourselves therefore to God. Resist the devil, and he will flee from you" (James 4:7).

I commanded the devil to leave my airspace. When I pray over our house and property, I include the airspace above our property and the ground beneath. I pray for mighty warring angels to surround our property. When an unbeliever sees the cross, I can tell it has an effect, but they do not quite understand why. Sometimes, when you're talking to someone about Jesus and when they physically see the cross, they start to get convicted. "Lest ye be drawn by the Father, ye cannot be saved" (John 6:44).

In the first epistle of John, it says, "If we say that we have no sin we deceive ourselves and the truth is not in us. If we confess our sins, He is faithful and just to forgive our sins and cleanse us from all unrighteousness. If we say we have not sinned, we make Him a liar and His word is not in us." When you are exposed to Jesus, your heart starts to crack, and truth starts to penetrate the soul through the Word, which is the Lord Jesus Christ.

When sin is revealed, if you receive Jesus and confess your sins, he is faithful and just to forgive you of your sins and cleanse you from all unrighteousness. Until Jesus comes in, you won't see the sin. There are a lot of words but only one living Word. In John, it says, "The words that I speak unto you, they are spirit and they are life" (John 6:63).

"The letter killeth, but the spirit giveth life" (2 Corinthians 3:6). "Christ loved the church and gave Himself for it that He might sanctify and cleanse it with the washing of water by the Word, that He might present it to Himself a glorious church, not having spot or wrinkle, or any such thing, that it should be Holy and without blemish" (Eph.5:25–27).

"Wherewithal shall a young man cleanse his way by taking heed thereto according to thy word" (Psalm 119:9). "Thy word hath quickened me" (Psalm 119:50). "Thy word have I hide in my heart, that I might not sin against thee" (Psalm 119:11). "I will not forget thy word" (Psalm 119:16). "How sweet are thy words unto my taste! Yea, sweeter than honey to my mouth!" (Psalm 119:103). "Through thy precepts I get understanding: therefore I hate every false way" (Psalm 119:104).

The Word is truth when Jesus is connected to it. The real truth will put you in heavenly glory. The false truth is from the dark side and has (false) power, and millions are deceived. Its roots are planted in hell. The Bible says, "Therefore hell hath enlarged herself, and opened her mouth without measure: and their glory, and their multitude, and their pomp, and he that rejoiceth, shall descend into it" (Isaiah 5:14).

The Word of God is truth, or God would be a liar, and if God was a liar, all of creation, including us, would cease to exist. "If we say that we have not sinned, we make him a liar, and his word is not in us" (1 John 1:10). You can't run from the fact that we are dust that God breathed in, and we are just not all that. He knows when you sin, and you especially know when you sin. First John says the following:

> My little children, these things write I unto
> you, that ye sin not. And if any man sin, we have

an advocate with the Father, Jesus Christ the righteous: And he is the propitiation for our sins: and not for ours only, but also for the sins of the whole world. (1 John 2:1–2)

(*Propitiation* meaning: one who has paid the price for another)

This scripture clearly shows that just because you're a born-again believer does not mean you will not make a mistake and sin. The book of Romans says, "The wages of sin is death, but the gift of God is eternal life through Jesus Christ our Lord" (Romans 6:23). That's why we will die; even though we're born-again, we can still sin. We have to put the Word of God in on a regular basis, or we could get weak in the spirit.

The Bible says, "Man drinketh iniquity like water" (Job 15:16). It also says, "The heart is deceitful above all things, and desperately wicked: who can know it? I the Lord searcheth the heart…" (Jeremiah 17:9–10). One cannot even trust his own conscience. Only the Word of God gives reliable counsel. Reading the Word and memorizing the Word are important in this day and age; corruption is running rampant, sexual immorality being the worst, and at many levels, the enemy knows the weakness of man.

People are dying every minute on the globe. In one hundred years, every one that is twenty-five years old will be dead, but we don't think it will be us until we get sick. Then you start to worry about the condition of your soul. When you surrender to Jesus Christ, you don't have to sweat it. I personally can't wait to see what's on the other side.

Yes, I am a sinner saved by grace. When I stand before him, I'll plead the blood of Jesus on my soul. Just like the ark, coated with pitch within and without to keep out the wrath of God (the flood), so is your soul coated by the blood of Jesus. Just like the blood of a lamb that was put over the doorpost to keep the angel of death away, so will you be protected by the blood of the Lamb.

CHAPTER 7

Self-Defense in the Spirit

"He that dwelleth in the secret place of the Most High shall abide under the shadow of the Almighty" (Psalm 91:1). My conscious is continually with him. If I'm in his shadow, I'm close to him and connected to him. His shadow is connected to him and part of him. Like your shadow is part of you where you go, your shadow is right there. When you're in his light, your shadow will clearly be visible.

"I will say of the Lord He is my refuge and my fortress: my God; in Him will I trust" (Psalm 91:2). I can sleep in him in peace. The living water will quench my spiritual thirst. The bread of life will fill my longing heart, and I will put on the whole armor of God to stand against the enemy of my soul. When I put my trust in him, he will take care of my physical needs and guide me to make the right decisions through the Holy Ghost.

"Surely He will deliver me from the snare of the fowler, and the noisome pestilence" (Psalm 91:3). Just like the fowler snares birds for lunch, the enemy would like to snare you into sin so he can have you for lunch (This psalm is a written attack against the demon realm. Memorize this psalm, and don't be shy with it.) A noisome pestilence is a noxious, harmful, deadly, overwhelming disease. "He shall cover thee with his feathers, and under his wings shalt thou trust: his truth shall be thy shield and buckler" (Psalm 91:4).

Refer to the whole armor of God in Ephesians Chapter 6 to see the power you have over the enemy in the name of Jesus Christ.

There is a story of a mother hen that got caught in a barn fire. She died in the fire when they went to move her; they found her baby chicks alive under her. She kept them under the shadow of her wings, like Christ keeps his born-again believers safe if they will surrender to him.

The shield of faith will quench all the fiery darts of the enemy. "Thou shalt not be afraid for the terror by night…" There is a night demon by the name of Lilith, which we rebuke in the name of the Lord Jesus Christ. Neither "…nor for the arrow that flieth by day" (Psalm 91:5). That's why we hold up the shield of faith; we are covered by the blood of Jesus, and our name is written in the Lamb's book of life.

"Nor for the pestilence that walketh in darkness." This could be the demon Namtar, and we rebuke this thing and plead the blood of *Jesus* and send this evil spirit back to hell. "Nor for the destruction that wasteth at noon-day" (Psalm 91:6). There is always that one-eyed demon that is always looking for trouble; we'll just call it Cyclops and stick a cross in its eye and kick it back to the lake of fire.

In March of 2021, on the news, it showed hundreds of young adults at spring break. It was on the evening; they had their smartphones as high as they could get them, trying to record everything they could. They would be lost without their smartphone. It controls their very life. I think the Lord was trying to tell me that it is the one-eyed demon that wastes at noon day.

"A thousand shall fall at thy side, and ten thousand at thy right hand; but it shall not come nigh thee" (Psalm 91:7). Isaiah 41:13 says, "For I the Lord thy God will hold thy right hand, saying unto thee, fear not, I will help thee." When everything is caving in around you, fear not death for the Lord Jesus Christ lives in you.

I really think the Lord will let us see the devil and his angels be cast into the lake of fire. That will be their reward. "Only with thine eyes shalt thou behold and see the reward of the wicked" (Psalm 91:8). "Because thou hast made the Lord, which is my refuge…" He is the tower that I run into. You must abide in the vine, and safety will be yours. "…Even the most High, thy habitation" (Psalm 91:9); Ephesians says that we are "in heavenly places in Christ Jesus…"

(Ephesians2:6). "There shall no evil befall thee, neither shall any plague come nigh thy dwelling" (Psalm 91:10).

We pray that the Spirit of the living God would surround our home and our property, the airspace above, and the ground beneath and surround it with mighty warring angels. "For he shall give his angels charge over thee, to keep thee in all thy ways. They shall bear thee up in their hands, lest thou dash thy foot against a stone" (Psalm 91:11–12).

When you read this, it's pretty clear that we have a guardian angel, but if you're not a born-again believer, I shudder to think the angel that is following you probably has a pitch fork around it. "Thou shalt tread upon the lion and adder." The lion is the most feared in the African jungle largely because it has a loud roar. The female does most of the hunting, and the male just acts like he is somebody around the girls, but don't underestimate him. He still seeks whom he may devour.

The adder, on the other hand, lies on the footpath and waits for you to step on him, and then he strikes without warning. It is most dangerous to the elderly and children (the most vulnerable). Doesn't that sound like Satan? Young lions still bite and claw, no matter how young they are, but the most dangerous is the dragon. It attacks the mind and heart; that's why we keep him under our feet and keep a life of prayer (Psalm 91:13).

"Because he hath set his love upon me, therefore will I deliver him: I will set him on high, because he hath known my name" (Psalm 91:14). His name is at my exhale and the breath that I take. "He shall call upon me, and I will answer him: I will be with him in trouble." This does not mean he will pull you out of the trouble, but he will be right there with you to make sure you get through it. He will honor you for not giving up. "With long life will I satisfy him, and show him my salvation" (Psalm 91:15–16). Jesus is the air that I breathe.

CHAPTER 8

Blessed of Revelation

"Blessed is he that readeth, and they that hear the words of this prophecy, and keep those things which are written therein: for the time is at hand" (Revelation 1:3). Yes, the time is at hand; look around you in just America alone. Churches are struggling to stay alive.

"And here is the patience of the saints: here are they that keep the commandments of God and the faith of Jesus" (Revelation 14:12). Small churches dot the land, and a small remnant keeps the spirit alive and will be faithful to the end, and the local pastor will see to it.

> And I heard a voice from heaven saying
> unto me, Write, Blessed are the dead which die
> in the Lord from henceforth: Yea, saith the Spirit,
> that they may rest from their labours; and their
> works do follow them. (Revelation 14:13)

Yes, when you become a born-again believer, your outlook on life changes; going to work early in the morning doesn't seem as bad as it used to be. Your fellow workers will say, "What's wrong with that guy?" They don't know that death for you now means you will pass from one dimension to another in the blink of an eye, and there will be no pain. "Behold, I come as a thief. Blessed is he that watcheth, and keepeth his garments, lest he walk naked, and they see his shame" (Revelation 16:15).

In these last days, we must keep our garments clean and white and put on the whole armor of God to deal with the dark side in the spiritual and learn how to defend yourself in the physical. One thing is true, in every day of our born-again experience, we'll have to put on the whole armor of God and battle against the devil and his angels. In Ephesians, it says the following:

> Finally, my brethren, be strong in the Lord, and in the power of his might. Put on the whole armor of God that ye may be able to stand against the wiles of the devil. For we wrestle not against flesh and blood, but against principalities, against powers, against the rulers of the darkness of this world, against spiritual wickedness in high places. (Ephesians 6:10–12)

"For though we walk in the flesh, we do not war after the flesh: (for the weapons of our warfare are not carnal, but mighty through God to the pulling down of strong holds.)" (2 Corinthians 10:3). "And after these things I heard a great voice of much people in heaven, saying, Alleluia; Salvation, and glory, and honor, and power unto the Lord our God" (Revelation 19:1).

> And a voice came out of the throne, saying, Praise our God, all ye his servants, and ye that fear him, both small and great. And I heard as it were the voice of many waters, and as a voice of mighty thunderings, saying, Alleluia: for the Lord God omnipotent reigneth. Let us be glad and rejoice, and give honor to him: for the marriage supper of the Lamb is come, and his wife hath made herself ready. And to her was granted that she should be arrayed in fine linen, clean and white: for the fine linen is the righteousness of saints. And he saith unto me, Write, Blessed are they which are called unto the marriage supper of

the Lamb. And he saith unto me, "These are the true sayings of God." (Revelation 19:5–9)

Teaching self-defense for over forty years, I tell my students that they are training for a physical battle here on earth and a spiritual battle after Jesus Christ takes them to glory, but the only weapon you'll need then is the Word of God. "And the armies which were in heaven followed him upon white horses, clothed in fine linen, white and clean" (Revelation 19:14).

> And Enoch also, the seventh from Adam, prophesied of these, saying, Behold, the Lord cometh with ten thousands of his saints, to execute judgment upon all. And to convince all that are ungodly among them of all their ungodly deeds which the ungodly have committed, and of all their hard speeches which ungodly sinners have spoken against him. (Jude: 14–15)

Yes, it is the Word that wins that battle. Revelation 20:4 says the following:

> And I saw thrones, and they sat upon them, and judgment was given unto them: and I saw the souls of them that were beheaded for the witness of Jesus, and for the word of God, and which had not worshipped the beast, neither his image, neither had received his mark upon their foreheads, or in their hands; and they lived and reigned with Christ a thousand years.

> But the rest of the dead lived not again until the thousand years were finished. This is the first resurrection. Blessed and holy is he that hath part in the first resurrection: on such the second death hath no power, but they shall be priests of God

and of Christ, and shall reign with him a thousand years. (Revelation 20:5–6)

Take one note that at the end of the thousand years, Satan will be loosed for a short season to tempt man, so keep your linen white and clean, and never drop your guard.

To explain the second death, as humans, we all will die (unless you're raptured). The second death is eternal separation from God and the torment of hell, if you're not saved, by rejecting Jesus Christ as your personnel savior.

The first chapter of Revelation starting with verses 9–11 says the following:

> I John, who also am your brother, and companion in tribulation and in the kingdom and patience of Jesus Christ, was in the isle that is called Patmos, for the testimony of Jesus Christ. I was in the Spirit on the Lord's Day, and heard behind me a great voice, as of a trumpet, saying, I am Alpha and Omega, the first and the last.

John stated, in Revelation 21:1, 4, "And I saw a new heaven and a new earth: for the first heaven and the first earth were passed away; and there was no more sea. And God shall wipe away all tears from their eyes; and there shall be no more death, neither sorrow, nor crying, neither shall there be any more pain: for the former things are passed away." And John said the following:

> He shewed me a pure river of life, clear as crystal, proceeding out of the throne of God and of the Lamb. In the midst of the street of it, and on either side of the river, was the tree of life, which bare twelve manner of fruits, and yielded her fruit every month: and the leaves of the tree were for the healing of the nations. (Revelation 22:1–2)

God said, "Behold I come quickly: blessed is he that keepeth the sayings of the prophecy of this book" (Revelation 22:7).

> And, behold I come quickly; and my reward is with me, to give every man according as his works shall be. I am Alpha and Omega, the beginning and the end, the first and the last. Blessed are they that do his commandments, that they may have right to the tree of life, and may enter in through the gates of the city. (Revelation 22:12–14)

It's clear that the Book of Revelation is sometimes hard to understand. It's also clear that the seven blessed of Revelation tell you that if you're a born-again believer, you will escape the wrath of Almighty God. Lord, come quickly!

CHAPTER 9

Sexual Immoralities and Addictions

(Note: This chapter is written from a different author. Due to the contents, the author prefers to remain anonymous.)

This chapter is about sexual addictions and sexual immoralities.

There are many levels of sexual addictions. If you have ever heard of the saying "new levels, new devils," it certainly applies to this subject. I will get into more detail later on in the chapter.

My ex-husband had a sexual addiction problem when we were married, and I figured that I'm probably a pretty good expert on how the other half comes out as a survivor and overcomer, living with a person that successfully hid ugly secrets for over twenty years of our marriage. If you recognize anything in this chapter that is in your life or know someone close to you that struggles with any degree of sexual immoralities, I pray this will open your spiritual eyes to get a glimpse of how this disease can ruin lives.

First thing that I want to get straight right from the beginning, in the Bible, you can find multiple verses that tell us that Jesus went around all the cities and villages, teaching, preaching, and healing every sickness and every disease. So a person can be healed from sexual addiction.

When I told my daughter that I was going to write a chapter in Ted's book, she was watching me intently when my emotions were changing, just by bringing up an old subject. I told her that I was going to pull my old journal out and reread it to remember the details that I have forgotten over the years. She said, "Why, Mom? Why would you open all that stuff up again?" I told her that Satan meant all that happened for evil, but God is going to get the glory out of it.

If I can help one person, this chapter will be worth writing it. My goal in doing this is to help save a person with addictions, not to destroy their lives and their families due to sexual addictions like it did to our family. Throughout this chapter, I plan on sharing pieces of letters that I have written and journal with you for some understanding of the darkness and sadness that enter in the home when addictions are present.

Leroy and I dated for one and a half years before we married. I knew on our third date that he was the man I was going to marry one day. When we got married, I knew it was going to be my forever. The thing that I didn't realize was that he had been addicted to porn since he was a teenager.

You probably are asking yourself, how I could have lived with someone for twenty-four years and not know something was wrong. Hopefully, you will understand the answer to this question sooner than it took me after reading my story.

I had just rededicated my life to Christ and was starting my marriage. My first memory of his pornography/sexual addiction was right after we first got married; I was looking through the attic and found crates, boxes, and stacks of magazines. When I asked him about them, he stated to me that they belonged to an old roommate that had lived there. It didn't seem to faze him when I threw them all out, so I didn't take any thought that he was lying to me.

At another time, he did want to introduce X-rated films to our marriage, but after seeing the contents of this film, it literally made me sick to my stomach, and I would not allow it back into my house again. Little did I know, it never left. I just didn't see it again till later when our three-and-a-half-year-old daughter found a film by mistake mixed in with her cartoon tapes.

We had been married for ten years by then. It was titled as the *Super Bowl*, so I didn't realize what it really contained. Another time, I found a receipt of a film that he had rented in his truck. It was obvious by seeing the title of what type of film it was. His excuse was that he gave a friend a ride, and he must have left it.

Over the years, these random occurrences happened repeatedly. His lies kept the secrets well hidden, but the addiction took on a life in my husband, and it grew. It started to manifest itself, and Leroy was changing. He grew angry, and he has expressed that he was no longer in love with me. We had been married for nineteen years.

We continued to live together but separately. I was still committed to him, and I still honored the vows that I took before God when we got married. Till death do us part. The only reason biblically that we could divorce was for adultery. I didn't trust him in a lot of things, but that was one thing I knew he would never do.

When the anger and verbal and mental abuse started more frequent, I knew our marriage was in trouble, but I didn't know why and where it was coming from. He would seek me out to belittle or pick a fight with me over trivial matters. There were times that he didn't make sense of the statements he would make. Things were said that he imagined in his mind.

I became scared for him, wondering if there was something mentally wrong. I suggested to him that I was worried about him, and some of the things that he was saying didn't make any sense. He then accused me of calling him crazy. I didn't know what was wrong with my husband, and he wouldn't get help. Everything was my fault.

I cooked like my mother. I kept my house too clean. I wore the wrong clothes. One day, as I was cleaning, he threw dirt and old mouse feces from a dustpan in my face and told me that I deserved it. There was something wrong with this man that I loved, and I was going to find out what it was.

The following journal entries are from my actual journal that I have put away. They were written near the end of our marriage when things got worse. Instead of seeking a counselor, I would journal letters to Leroy when I could no longer talk to him. I didn't feel safe.

Journal (letter written to him but not given—2004): *In the middle of the night, I wake up and your pillow is empty. I wake up from a dream or a nightmare, your pillow is empty. Before I go to sleep and just need to be held, the pillow is empty. Years of this…my heart is empty. I'm so lonely when you are there now. The only way to get you to be home was to threaten you. I had to make rules for you to go by. It was my last resort to force you home hoping you would come back to us. I hate all the other lovers (porn websites) you have had in the past. It is not the things itself, but your willingness to put them before us. The lover you have now, I'm jealous. You are cheating on me and cheating me from being with you. I am so angry with you for that and the secret you have kept from me for years doing that. I still can't stop crying when I think about our marriage. I'm still looking for hope. Is it too late? I still can't see hope. It's got to be there somewhere. My heart is broken, but I don't know if I have enough to put it back together. I love you so much and I know you love me in some ways. Is that enough? If you would tell me that you love me, it might make me cry, but in those tears would be a mixture of healing tears and some pain that I let out so your affection and love can take its place. The weird thing about it is that it still hurts when you do show affection, but it heals also. That's why I emotionally push you away at this point. I'm so overfilled with hurt, anger and loss; attention makes those feeling surface also.*

Journal (letter written to him but not given—2004): *After you left the bedroom last night, I broke down, sobbing. Then my Father in Heaven spoke one word to me. He said, "Wait." "Wait? Wait on what?" I asked. He said "Wait on me, for I am God." After He said that, the Holy Spirit took over as I began to pray. He gave me boldness. Boldness I haven't had in a while. I was shivering because of my nerves and of coldness, but a warmth came over me. I started speaking to Satan. I told him that he has no business in my home, he has no business with my husband, he has no business with my daughter, and he has no business with me. I told him with the authority of the Holy Spirit to get out of my house, get away from my family and get away from my marriage. I told him to be far removed and never come back; he has no authority here in the name of Jesus. This house is sanctified under the blood of Jesus. Get out! Do you hear me? Get out! Don't you ever come back in the name of Jesus!*

Leroy, if you only learn one thing through this, I want you to know, I have prayed for our marriage and I will not go down without a fight. I believe this will one day lead you to God with a relationship with Him also.

After these journal letters, things did get better, then worse. Leroy and I were currently in counseling for his anger and temper. I was finding out more of the extent of the sexual addictions he was involved in from me secretly digging into computer history/cookies, visiting our local movie rental store, looking into our phone records, and occasional spying on him late at night when he thought I was asleep.

I was waiting to confront him with the counselor present. I was afraid of him at that point, and I didn't know what he was capable of doing.

During one of our counseling sessions, I had expressed that I felt closed off from Leroy. When he did try to approach me to hold me, I wouldn't put my arms around him; I crossed my arms in front of my chest. I was in self-protection mode but not realizing what I was doing. The counselor suggested allowing myself to open up and put my arms around Leroy.

So one day, Leroy was standing at the sink and washing dishes when I came up behind him and put my arms around him and touched his arms.

I asked him, "So how's it feel washing dishes?"

He then pulled a knife out of the dishwater and asked, "How would it feel to have a knife in your back?"

Who was this man? He was a stranger to me.

The pastoral counselor led Leroy in the salvation prayer, and he accepted Jesus as his savior. I had a glimmer of hope now. I knew Leroy, and I didn't have to fight our issues alone. That didn't last long though. Leroy eventually turned his back on God. Everything surfaced to the top, and I confronted him shortly after that.

We were in our marriage counseling session. I had just gone to the video store and picked up a copy of the movie history. I asked Leroy when was the last time he watched porn. He stated that it had been months. I told him that he was a liar. I then told the counselor that Leroy was lying to both of us. I then read off the movies he had just rented two days prior. Leroy was angry…as expected.

Journal (partial letter written to Leroy—5/2005): *When we fell in love, I knew it was going to be forever. I trusted you and loved you almost immediately after we met. You were the one that I was looking for in a husband and to spend the rest of my life with.*

Even after everything I have found out recently, it still seems to be a bad dream and I was going to wake up and minute and find that none of this is true. I really can't understand how something can get ahold of someone so strong that they can lie to the one that they say they love. Now, I question how much of our marriage and our life together was real and what was a lie. What was the truth in our marriage? I can't separate the two. As angry as I am with you right now, I also feel sorry for you and worried about you. Please get the help you need! If it took me confronting you, and you realizing our marriage is in jeopardy to finally face this, it will be to your benefit in the long run. Don't escape into it further; it will ruin your life, like it has done to ours. It's hard to say goodbye to you and maybe I'm not ready for that yet, but I don't even know who you are! How much of our marriage was real and how much is fake?

I need to make plans for my future. Who knows, maybe one day or even years we can try again. That is probably unrealistic thinking, because at this point, I don't know how I can ever get over all this baggage we have. I can't separate the lies from the truth. Maybe one day you can tell me that what I thought was love for me was real or not. No one will ever love you the way I have and that is why I am so hurt and feel so betrayed. I kept believing you even though I knew something wasn't right. That's what a wife does. She believes in her husband.

As I think, over the years, you have felt that your life is out of your control, probably stems mostly from your addiction. So, you waited for me to request changes to take place, thinking maybe you would get peace; instead only resentment and anger would come instead. Of course, most of it would be targeted towards me.

Your anger has not been about me, it's been about your lack of control, guilt, resentment and anger towards yourself. I can't fix, what I didn't break; but, I became a wounded victim in the middle of this. For my own mental health, I need to find closure in this. I miss you so desperately. You have no idea how painful this is for me. I keep going back and forth with my decision, but I can't live under the same roof with someone who is so angry with me when I haven't done anything wrong.

I am naturally a peacemaker. I want to step in and fix other people's problems. That's why I keep wavering on my decision. I want to fix you, but I can't. Only you can make that decision and not because I want you to! To gain your own self-respect, you need to accomplish this. I will do anything I can to help you, but you need to ask me. I will no longer step in and make decisions for you. Everything is up to you now.

Our daughter and I had moved out of our home. Leroy and I thought that if I didn't live there, we could start all over again. We would date again, and we were hoping his anger with me would subside.

Insert of letter to pastoral counselor (5/2005): *...I believe Leroy needs this immediately (specialized counseling), especially since his ground is ready to receive and to be seeded (Mat.13:23) at this time. He needs to face this head on! For these reasons is why I am writing this letter to you instead of attending our session. He needs to be concentrating on getting to the root of this addiction. He couldn't have just woke up one morning and started to do this to himself (self-harm) on a daily basis without reason...*

After that, I no longer went to counseling with Leroy. Leroy went from counselor to counselor. He would become angry with each one and then change to a different counselor. He never talked about what happened during the sessions.

Journal (letter written to him but not given—6/2005): *I made up my mind. I decided. No more. I pushed and pushed. Begged and pleaded. Threatened and set curfews. (Note: He would not come home till late at night; and we did not know where he was. I told him to be at home to at least kiss his daughter goodnight.) Everything that I had tried; I then think of something else and tried it. I was losing the battle. I was fighting for something you weren't wanting. I was fighting for your love and you weren't willing to give it to me. I would stay awake at night and wonder what the pieces that were missing were. I knew I was doing everything I could think of. I was a good wife, a good mother, helped provide for our family the best way I knew how. I supported you in any dream that you had. Even putting off my dream, so you could fulfill yours. I hate you for making me lose everything. My marriage, my home and was never your first love. I have our daughter though. I have raised her right.*

She has turned out so wonderful, but how much damage have you caused her? Her way of thinking; especially about men in her life?!

The crazy thing is that I miss you. I don't know what I miss about though. You have made my life miserable so many times. When there were good times, you were doing other things (porn, etc.) the whole time! So, you weren't even being loyal to me then. So, when were the good, happy times? Were any of them real. Were you thinking of others when you were with me? You have so betrayed me! So, what part of this do I miss?

It's true you know. The vows we took. Two become as one. That's been the painful part for me. It's the ripping and tearing apart. It's not an even cut; the tearing has jagged tears. They don't heal so easy and there is part of my body missing. When I do try to talk to you, you still seem so angry with me. At least sympathize with me a little. Be angry with yourself, not me! You would be having a hard time with this also if you found out that I was having an affair that has lasted 23 years also! And…lying countless lies to cover it up! Not loyal one day of our marriage! Try that on for size! It leaves a real bad taste in one's mouth! Then, you have the audacity to be angry with me!? To even act angry, or look at me with anger? How dare you!

It's still so hard to let you go. I know that I need to, but I'm having a real hard time letting go. At least you could have compassion for me instead of contempt. Do you think any of your actions toward me now is going to draw me to you? Or, are you acting like this to push me away even further?

Journal (8/1/05): *A lot has happened since my last letter and also nothing has happened at all. My emotions have definitely been on a roller coaster ride in the last 3 months and a lot of healing from God has taken place. If I could see all the tears I have spilled, it would probably amaze even me. Every tear that has fallen has been a healing balm to my soul and spirit. Never in my life did I ever think I would have had this tough of a trial to go through. It literally pulled the bottom out of my life! I thought it was hard before not know what was wrong, but now that I know the magnitude of it, it has been way too overwhelming. (Note: Things that is still too personal to write about that I need to exclude) I thank God for his healing. It hasn't happened overnight, but he has done it in the timing that he has seen fit. I had to go thru all the stages of loss, shock, hurt, anger, disappointment and reality of this. I don't ever want to feel acceptance, because I will never accept it the way things are now. I know these problems are real and I am determined to keep going and to find peace and joy in the midst of my troubles. God will be the only one to give me this. How can people merely live on their own? I can't imagine being alone thru this. The crazy thing is, that I probably feel more peace now then I have in years. This must come from God, my father.*

I still have so many questions not answered yet. I have forgiven Leroy. I see parts of him sometimes come out. He is showing emotions that I have never seen before. He tears up at just about every church service he attends. I know God is getting through to him. If he would just stop fighting against God, He will finish the work in Leroy. I guest Leroy has a process that he has to go thru also. I wish I could help him, but he needs to make these baby steps on his own. Leroy has been crippled for so long (emotionally), he needs to learn how to walk again. Just like a baby, it takes time.

What happens when he does recover? Do I go back? I fear his anger and temper. That has been such a big part of him. Will that ever go away? Will he still blame me for things? Will he continually be negative and critical of everything? Do I have to go back since we are married? Would I be wrong if I didn't? Right now, I still feel repulsed by his actions (self-satisfaction). Will that ever go away?

God told me to wait. I pray all my questions will be answered soon. It's always in God's timing and I know I can't rush Him. It sure is tough being patient.

Journal (8/6/05): *It is increasingly getting harder to wait. I don't see an end to this anytime soon. When I asked Leroy about coming back home (daughter and I are living with my parents), he clearly wasn't ready for us to try again. Even when we are getting along, I still don't hear from him. I wonder if we didn't go to church every Sunday together, how often I would see him. I fear he is slipping further away from me and I don't know how to stop it. He clearly still has a lot to work out in himself, but don't we all have issues to deal with? We learn to cope. Maybe he cannot cope with all the responsibilities it takes to be a husband, father and head of the household. Maybe, he never will. I need to adjust to the fact he may never want us back.*

What happened to my husband? This man is a shell of who Leroy used to be. He has an illness which I'm not sure if wants a cure. All his responsibilities will be required of him again. Does he want it? Can he do it? Even though, I have worked thru most of the anger and I have forgiven him, I still feel a part of me is missing. It's probably like an amputee missing a limb, but can still feel it even though it is gone. I miss my other half no matter what he has done to me. I feel such a loss.

I'm tired of waiting God; but I have no choice, do I?

After I confronted Leroy in front of the counselor, the counselor told me that Leroy couldn't help himself. He called it a "sickness from the evil one." I knew that this pastoral counselor was over his head in helping Leroy when he was making excuses for Leroy. I wrote the counselor a letter stating that Leroy needed specialized counseling in sexual addiction and reminded him what the Word of God tells me.

I asked him, "Doesn't it say in the Word that we always have a way of escape? Satan does tempt us, but we are drawn away from our own lusts" (*James 1:14*). I also reminded him of 1 Corinthians 10:13: "There hath no temptation taken you but such as is common to man: but God is faithful, who will not suffer you to be tempted above that ye are able; but will with the temptation also make a way to escape, that ye may be able to bear it."

He did ask our daughter and me to come home shortly after this last journal entry. I told him that now that I know of his pornography and sexual addictions, we can struggle together. I had boundaries though that he needed to agree with, or I couldn't move back home. One of them was no more lying and deception. I expected him to slip, but he needed to talk to me, and we can struggle together. He agreed.

It lasted six weeks. We moved out again, but we still came over to visit. I was still paying all the bills and taking care of our pets. One evening, there was an unfamiliar jeep in the driveway and a woman's purse in the living room. I didn't get the opportunity to meet the person who owned the purse because Leroy made me leave the house.

As months went on, it was like puzzle pieces falling out of nowhere and starting to form a picture of the past twenty-three years. More pieces came together as the secrets came to a head.

I asked the Lord one day, "Why now? Why now are you showing this to me?"

He answered, "Because you weren't ready before."

Our divorce was one year later.

It has taken me fifteen years to publicly talk about this because it has been a process of healing, forgiveness, and letting go of the hurt, anger, and deep-rooted bitterness that has been hiding in my heart. The betrayal has been the worst part of the emotional baggage that I came away with when we finally parted ways and divorced. I can honestly say I'm still not sure that I don't have more healing to come yet.

Every once in a while, a trigger will pop up on me and take me by surprise. I have become hypersensitive when someone raises their voice at me. It's also difficult to watch a movie with any content of a wife being abused in any way. Do you remember those old *Get Smart* shows where Maxwell Smart is a secret agent and they go to a dungeon/vault where his office is?

All kinds of doors close, one right after another; big metal doors come up from the ground, while one comes down from the top to meet it in the center. Doors from the sides meet in the middle as Maxwell goes into his inner chambers; then he finally disappears in some sort of elevator shaft or something.

The triggers are not to that extreme, but all the same, I created the walls around my heart for protection and actively fight it daily (spiritually and emotionally). With all that being said, I call myself a survivor and learned the meaning of being a real prayer warrior during the twenty-four years of marriage I was with Leroy. My Lord God has been and continues to be and still is my healer.

You see, it wasn't about the bad marriage. It wasn't about that we couldn't get along. The betrayal killed us. He sought other women, whether it was a computer, lingerie catalog, porn magazine, or another woman. It was cheating and adultery.

Our marriage was over because of the magazine that he picked up when he was just a teenage boy. I was willing to forgive him of his cheating, but he had to stop the porn. He chose the porn instead. He once told me that I was too much work.

Sexual addiction is a disease. It has many facets and stages as many other diseases. For example, in certain cancers, there are four stages of cancer. As the disease progresses, so does the stage. Sexual addiction can eat away the body as well. There are three levels of sexual additions. It can also affect the mind as I have witnessed.

This addiction can also cause death in many cases, depending on the stage in the addiction. Extreme cases of sexual addictions are just as lethal as the other deadly diseases that are more well-known.

There are three levels of sexual addictions, but you don't have to reach the third level like cancer before it will kill you. You can cause great harm to yourself and others in the first level:

- Level 1: masturbation, porn, prostitution, etc.
- Level 2: exhibitionism, voyeurism, indecent phone calls, etc.
- Level 3: child molestation, incest, rape, etc.

There are many books available that can give you a better understanding of sexual addictions.

When you think of someone with a sexual addiction, it is generally thought of men. Unfortunately, this disease does not have a gender or age preference. It doesn't have a status symbol. It doesn't care if you are rich or poor. Anyone can be pulled into this.

The church that I used to attend has this 24-7 prayer phone, which we got calls from all over the United States for people calling in need of prayer. A few years ago, it was our turn to have the phone. I answered it one evening, and it was a pastor's wife needing prayer for her husband that was addicted by pornography. She was so scared that someone in her church would find out and it would tear the church apart.

I believe God intervened that night in our prayers for her husband, their marriage, and their church. I still think about her. I am familiar with the deep sorrow, shame, and burden she carried. She is the victim in that story.

With the Internet so accessible, this secret can be kept private and hidden for many years if pornography is his/her only stage in this disease. Eventually, secrets do find a way of coming out. As the disease progresses, it can and will affect others. It could be other relationships, your spouse, or your children. It can reach out to the community and strangers that can become victims.

You only need to turn the TV on for just a few minutes, and usually, there is something on the news that can be associated with some sort of sexual addiction. As I mentioned earlier, there are so many facets and stages. It could start out as simple as a lingerie magazine or catalog.

I read several years ago that pornography in particular is so addictive that you can become addicted after viewing porn one time. If that is true, that's just addictive as heroin or any strong opioid. That seed was planted for a taste of just a little more and can go in so many directions after that. Do they have a taste for a same-sex relationship, multiple partners, or opposite sex partners outside of their current relationship? What about child pornography?

This epidemic is running rapid in the country so much so that people are visiting other countries to seek children sex slaves. Not only in other countries but also it is an epidemic of children and adults that are disappearing into sex slavery in the United States to satisfy the unrelinquished hunger of sexual addictions.

This is just the beginning of sexual deviations people can fall into. There are other limbs that branch out due to sexual addictions. To list a few more: sexual suicides by suffocations, same-sex relationships, and self-harm for sexual pleasures. These are all types of perversions or transgressions. The list goes on.

Many people may not agree with me that same-sex relationships can be tied into the topic that I am discussing, but I would defiantly disagree every time. I don't believe a baby, created by God, would be mistakenly given the wrong gender they were intended to have. That would tell me that God made a mistake.

I believe somewhere along the way in the child's life, their identity was interrupted somehow, whether it was molestation, the home environment, or the child's thought process and development that changed in another direction. I really don't have the answer, but I'm one of the people who believe a person wasn't born that way. I don't expect everyone to be in agreement with me on that. The Bible is very clear on the topic of same-sex relations. Why would God create a child born with those tendencies when he clearly states it is an abomination in his Word.

The Bible has everything we need. The Word of God has all the contents to prevent this lifestyle from starting; it has multiple examples of people and cities that were infested with these sins, and it has a way of escaping and healing. The amazing thing is, God is present at all times to be there when we need him.

How do we prevent this lifestyle? It starts with the eyes. Looking empowers lust, which is never love. We should never look unto things that can lead us into impurity. It opens the doors to numerous sins: manipulation, lies, and deception. It affects marriages. A person develops the wrong appetite for cravings.

Matthew 6:22 states, "The light of the body is the eye: if therefore thine eye be single, thy whole body shall be full of light."

Psalms 101:3, 4 states, "I will set no wicked thing before mine eyes: I hate the work of them that turn aside; it shall not cleave to me. A froward heart shall depart from me: I will not know a wicked person." (Note: *froward* meaning: very perverse, crooked, distorted, warped)

Proverbs 27:20 states, "Hell and destruction are never full; so the eyes of man are never satisfied."

There are two words that I would like to focus on. The first is *iniquity*. When I looked this word up in a Bible dictionary, there are multiple meanings, but they are all common with each other, such as desire, craving, moral evil, moral perverseness, moral wrong, etc. It's basically lust if we want to condense all these meanings. When I looked it up in a concordance, there were literally hundreds of scriptures in reference to this word. It would be a great Bible study at another time.

So *iniquity* is basically an inward motivation toward sin in the heart, which in turn affects the family as you have read in my story. *Iniquity* goes from generation to generation: in 2 Samuel 11, David fell; in 2 Samuel 13, David's son fell.

Second Samuel 11:2 states, "…And from the roof he (David) saw a woman (Bathsheba) washing herself; and the woman was very beautiful to look upon."

Second Samuel 11:15 states, "And he (David) wrote in the letter, saying, Set ye Uriah (Bathsheba's husband) in the forefront of the hottest battle, and retire ye from him, that he may be smitten, and die."

Second Samuel 13:2 states, "And Amnon was so vexed, that he fell sick for his sister Tamar; for she was a virgin; and Amnon thought it hard for him to do any thing to her."

Second Samuel 13:14 states, "Howbeit he (Amnon) would not hearken unto her (Tamar, sister) voice; but, being stronger than she, forced her, and lay with her."

The second word is *transgression*. I never thought the two words were much different, but they have two complete meanings. The meaning to this word in a Bible dictionary is treachery, to break away from authority, revolt, wickedness, and breaking.

This word tells me that this is an action word. It is an outwardly action versus the word *iniquity*, which is an inward description. So when iniquity is present, transgressions show up.

> But he was wounded (outside) for our transgressions, he was bruised (inside) for our iniquities: the chastisement of our peace was upon him; and with his stripes we are healed. All we like sheep have gone astray; we have turned every one to his own way; and the Lord hath laid on him the iniquity of us all. (Isaiah 53:5, 6)

> The integrity of the upright shall guide them: but the perverseness of transgressors shall destroy them. Riches profit not in the day of

wrath: but righteousness delivereth from death. The righteousness of the perfect shall direct his way: but the wicked shall fall by his own wickedness. The righteousness of the right shall deliver them: but transgressors shall be taken in their own naughtiness. (Proverbs 11:3–6)

I don't have all the answers, and I hope one day Leroy's eyes will be opened up. The men and women that I have come in contact with these secret sins have one thing in common. They struggle. Once they opened that door to the lust of the flesh, it becomes difficult to be delivered from it.

One Christian man I know seems to think, just because of God's grace, God will look the other way. Leroy thought every man is the same, and it is perfectly normal to look at videos and pictures and have affairs. One woman I know cannot have certain channels in her programming because she knows she is weak in this area and will watch it.

I'm sure there are millions of stories and reasons why they excuse their sins or can't seem to be delivered. I know from experience that it is a difficult thing to live through and how it rips a family apart. It saddens me that Satan has blinded the eyes and hearts of many.

If you are challenged by this chapter or any of it sounds a little familiar, God is still our/your deliverer. He was wounded for our transgressions and bruised for our iniquities. There is hope in him.

By Anonymous

Ted: Now My Response to This Chapter

If a man or woman wants to view sexually explicit material and drawn to it, it is very dangerous; if you're a Christian, you're playing with fire. Throw some ice on it before it gets a hold on you. The Bible says, "We must be born of the water and the spirit to enter the kingdom of God, listen to the Spirit, and be continually washed by the water of the Word."

Jesus answered, "Verily, verily, I say unto thee, except a man be born of the water and the spirit, he cannot enter the Kingdom of God" (John 3:5). Porn is certainly sin (work of the flesh). "Now the works of flesh are manifest, which are these; adultery, fornication, uncleanness, lasciviousness" (Galatians 5:19).

Let's look at just lasciviousness. It describes a person's behavior driven by sex; it boils down to lust. If it's not your spouse, it's lust. If you're not a Christian, you may not understand this. You might think its natural…only if you're a tomcat. If you're married, it's called adultery. The lifestyle of homosexuality is a relationship of lust.

Like porn, it is a work of the flesh (lust); you cannot inherit the kingdom of God according to Galatians 5:19–21. We as men notice the beauty of a woman that is natural. If you're putting yourself with her in your mind sexually, it is sin unless she is your wife. An idle mind can be a dangerous thing; keep busy doing good things. If anything else, go fishing, or go split some wood.

Look at the Ten Commandments; they are still in effect in the year 2021. Repent and turn to this before it destroys you spiritually, mentally, physically, and financially. Find someone you can confide in and trust that will console you and hold you accountable and that is a true prayer warrior.

If you're a true born-again believer, you can turn from this, there is a way out, and his name is the Lord Jesus Christ. Ask the Holy Spirit for guidance, and pray without ceasing. Read and research Galatians 5:19–21. Find a Christian counselor and a qualified pastor and his wife to help you through this and hold you accountable. I'll always be praying for you.

Missions across the World

I joined the Navy just shortly out of high school. My dad was a World War II veteran, and he fought the Nazis in the European theater. He had five bronze stars, and he was basically a war hero with no purple heart. So I was motivated to follow in his footsteps.

My first long mission with the Navy was to the Mediterranean Sea. It was aboard the USS *Newman K Perry*, a 692 class destroyer. We crossed the Atlantic to the Azores Islands, and we needed fresh water as our distilling plants were malfunctioning, and not just the crew that needed water but our boilers required a lot of makeup feedwater to make steam due to the props that were driven by sixty-thousand-horsepower steam turbines.

I worked in the after-engine room at the bottom of the ship. We cruised through the Strait of Gibraltar. On the right, you could see Morocco and Africa and on the left, Gibraltar on the coast of Spain. We then went on to Naples, Italy. There, we saw many sites including castles. Off in the distance, we could clearly see Mt. Vesuvius, the volcano that destroyed Pompeii in AD 79.

We could stand on the deck of the ship and see that the volcano was smoking. We were hoping it would be quiet while we were there. The harbor was an ancient seaport and was filthy. When we made fresh water from their harbors, we had to add bleach to the water, so it was safe to drink.

We left Italy and stopped at Augusta Bay, Sicily, for a short visit then on to Barcelona, Spain, and other cities on the coast of Spain. The next stop was Mallorca and an island resort for some rest and relaxation. The next stops were Nice, France, and Cannes, France. Yes, it might look like we were on vacation, but we were on NATO exercises.

The Vietnam War was still going on, but we were in Europe to show the world that we, of the United States, could be everywhere all at the same time. We were also working with other nations and their Navies. We left Europe for the States. Soon after that, we headed north for Nova Scotia to Halifax and more naval maneuvers.

We then went back south to the Caribbean Sea and then to St. Thomas Virgin Island, Bahamas, and Puerto Rico for gunnery practices (They were preparing us for Vietnam.). We traveled to Guantanamo Bay, Cuba, for engineering drills. I've been to Guantanamo Bay three times and been through the Bermuda Triangle three times and survived a hurricane at sea.

While in the Caribbean, on our way to Roosevelt Roads, Puerto Rico, for liberty, our orders changed. A satellite picked up a Russian guided-missile destroyer and a Russian nuclear submarine leaving Havana, Cuba, and heading for the US territorial waters. We followed them for days. Once, we lost sonar contact with the sub.

I was on throttles in the after engine. I got an order for "all ahead flank." Then almost as fast as I got the first order, I got an "all stop" then "all back full." The submarine was right under us, and the sonar didn't pick it up. Then the nuclear submarine surfaced right in front of our ship approximately seventy-five yards. We came close to colliding with Soviet Russia. If we would have hit the submarine, it would have been an international incident, and a lot of sailors from both sides would not have made it.

The choices we make and how fast we make them could change the world. If the officer of the watch would not have done his job or if I would have controlled the steam to the main turbines to slow, there could have been a nuclear accident and lives lost. God had his hand on this situation and at that time in my life.

I didn't really know Jesus, but I know that our nation was praying for the men in uniform, like they always have. I was not saved at this point in my life but was told growing up that if I died while in active service in the military for my country, I would go to heaven. I carried a small Bible I got in boot camp when I flew.

In 1973, I went from active service to inactive reserve. For twenty more years, I served my country as a citizen sailor and went to sea or a naval base somewhere in the country every year till I retired from military service in 1995. I did not know anything about being saved but thought I was okay till I met a chaplain at the Naval Reserve Center in Mansfield, Ohio.

There, I heard a scripture I never heard before taught and preached like he did. It still took a few years before I got saved; the Word was working on me. I thought if I just did church stuff, I would be okay. Finally, the Word cracked my heart and entered in. The truth lies within, and the rest is history.

Now the real *mission* starts. In the year 2000, Matt, a guitar player, and myself in the praise-and-worship team left with five others, destination: Africa. At that time, I was going to the Victory Temple Church of God. The missionary group we went with was Flaming Fire Ministries from Bowling Green, Ohio. We flew to London, England. We had a day layover, so we visited the city.

London seemed dead (probably dead religion). We flew ten hours to Harare, Zimbabwe, and ministered to the people. We also went to Gweru, Zimbabwe, always spreading the gospel. The church we ministered in didn't have a roof yet. Brother Matt preached more often, but I was honored to speak a few times with an interpreter. I mostly went to carry equipment, water, and Bibles. I also did some of the cooking.

We were many times in the middle of nowhere, but Jesus was always with us. Wild animals were in the midst, but they didn't pay us a mind as long as we stayed out of their way.

We then leased a driver and van to take us to Lusaka, Zambia. You could hear the elephants and hyenas that were right outside our vehicle, and we could hear lions roaring all night. We spent the night at the Zimbabwe and the Zambia border. They shut the border down at night. The border was guarded by soldiers with AK-47s.

The main missionary said we would take one pill (the gospel). I did not know we should get shots for the trip; this was all new to me. I brought mosquito netting for the trip and was thankful that I brought extras for the rest of the group that was with me. We were deep into Africa, and we all wore them, but one of the missionaries still got malaria. The mosquitoes were really bad.

On our way to look at land to buy for an orphanage, we ran into a crowd of people gathered around a witch doctor and his drummer. Of course, they thought they were getting healed or that the witch doctor was casting out demons, but the witch doctor had the demon. We prayed, and through the blood of Jesus, we ran off this pack of demons and sent them back to the pit.

Then the people felt the real power of God. We then visited an orphanage; they fed the children and tried to take care of them. I picked up this one little girl and held her; she fell asleep almost immediately for about an hour during one of the services for the children. The children's ages ranged from babies to about seven years old, and a lot of the children were HIV-positive.

We then took a ten-hour bus ride through the jungle. Of course, the locals brought their animals and whatever else they could carry, with rest stops on the way; women were on one side of the bus and men on the other (third-world countries don't have toilet paper). You were hoping something in the jungle wouldn't drag you away for suppertime.

We visited a prison in Mongo, Zambia. The warden let us pray for the prisoners, and the conditions of the prison were terrible. We also visited a hospital that looked like a rundown garage; we prayed for people in the psychiatric ward. Then we went on to Kitwe, Zambia, where the hotels had insect nets over the beds instead of glass in the windows.

We visited a church where the Holy Spirit moved so much that when we prayed for them, they fell out in the Spirit. The whole congregation was lying on the floor. I'll never forget the singing and harmony of the African people, without hardly any musical instruments. When we got to Lusaka, Zambia, to fly out of Africa to go back to London, England, then to the States, we ran into a slight problem. Our visas were two days over our stay.

The custom agents wouldn't give us back our passports. We all held hands and started praying, some in tongues. The officials rushed out and gave us our passports, and we were homeward bound. That was in 2000. The next year, terrorists flew two airliners into the twin towers. I'm glad we went to Africa in 2000 because after the terrorists' attack, they ground all air travel.

The next mission was India in the year 2013. This trip was with *Far-Flung Tin Can* (Kyle Philippi, founder and director). This trip was harder to leave because I'm now a happily married man to Brenda, but the Lord said, "Go." When the Creator says, "Go," you better go. We left Chicago, Illinois, airport to London, England, then to Bangalore, India, then a train to Chennai, India, and believe me, until you ride a train in India, you've not ridden a train.

The air conditioner was out at the YMCA, so we got rooms at the Marriott Hotel. When I looked out the window, I noticed we were in a million-dollar hotel, and outside, they were living in poverty-level shacks and makeshift homes, but they didn't seem to mind. I think they just accept that is what they are born into and that they can't do anything about it. But guess what, we brought Jesus; they just don't know it yet.

The water in India was not good enough to drink, so we brought our own and had to buy water. We would be going through a lot of water; it was at least one hundred degrees and a hundred-percent humidity. We had to be careful not to drink the water we were showering with in the hotel; it could even make you sick. We prepared for those things, but weren't going to take chances.

We were soon at the Home of Love, orphanage in Chennai, India. There were over ninety girls there and mostly children. It is a Christian sanctuary in the middle of 85 percent Hindu populations. If you look up Home of Love, Chennai, India, you'll see where we were; they could use your donation. The children were unbelievable: so full of freedom and love. Truly, Jesus Christ was in this place.

We soon bonded with the children. The older girls would catch a bus to a school outside the walls of Home of Love. Yes, the Home of Love orphanage was surrounded by a wall to keep the children and staff safe. The younger children were in class throughout the day. Do you know that you can sponsor a child at the Home of Love?

I was the oldest of our group, and the children called me grandfather. The fact is, I might be the only grandfather they will ever know. The staff was incredible. They made sure that we had everything we needed and fed us well. I didn't care much for the curry, but when in Rome, do as the Romans do. Kyle and one of the ladies were left-handed, but in India, you cannot eat with your left hand; it was fun watching them adjust.

Even though I went basically for security reasons, the Lord had me there to pray us through each day and carry equipment and mostly water. The rest of the crew was busy with all kinds of duties. I could feel the warfare of the enemy throughout the night, but we are overcomers by the blood of the Lamb and the word of our testimony.

The biggest reason for being there was to film the *Unwanted Treasure*, which there are fifty million girls missing from the country of India, filmed to raise moneys for the Invisible Girl Project. There are temples everywhere, Hindu mostly, and then there is Islam and a very small percentage of Christian. There is always a remnant; the remnant is the truth, and that makes it the most powerful.

We went in town, where a lady came to Chennai years ago and never left. She started a place where troubled girls and women could get help to learn a trade and get medical help, even women with HIV-positive conditions. I got a picture with them and bought a flower. They put flowers together to make money. This place also worked with a leaper colony in the area. I bought a book about the lady that started this organization, and she autographed it.

A small group of us took a train to Madurai in Southern India. We got with a group that helps people to keep their little girls, to help them to learn how to raise money so they don't sell the girls, with some outside funding for them. This was a sad experience, but we saw hope for the future. I prayed for a lot of people even though they were Hindu; they still received the prayer.

When we met up with the rest of the group a few days later, we visited the site where St. Thomas hid and prayed in a cave. Saint Thomas brought the gospel to India and was later martyred there. He was killed by a spear in the back. See, Satan was afraid to face him.

On these trips, Kyle always sees to it that we see the sites like the temples and the Bay of Bengal. We even played cricket. They thought we were professionals; now, you know that's true! What a trip, with not much sleep and a lot of praying day and night. Children are the same all over the world. They know what real love is. Now, the long flight back to Shelby, Ohio, USA.

The next mission was the Amazon rainforest, five hundred miles into Brazil, on a small ship with fifty-three people down the Amazon River. Its 2018, and I am catching a plane out of Cleveland, Ohio, to Detroit, Michigan, then to Washington, DC, where we met up with others bound for Miami, Florida. There is where we met up with the whole *Far-Flung Tin Can* crew.

Checking in and out of all these airports was some experience. With customs, there are so many regulations because of terrorism. It's best to know what you can and cannot take on an airplane because they will keep it. Make sure you have your passport and visa up-to-date.

Now that we were all together, we flew to Manaus, Brazil, where we found our small ship docked a ways from where the bus dropped us off. We carried our luggage through a maze and boarded our ship. We traveled three days to the first village. We slept outside in hammocks. It took all three days to figure out how to sleep in those things. I had a mosquito net to fit on the hammock. This was the adventure of a lifetime.

When the ship rocked, we all rocked the same direction. When we got to the village, we met the chief and got permission to minister to the villages. Teams went to the surrounding villages, ministering to the locals. Many healings and miracles happened. The teams were in boats with holes in the bottoms and no life jackets. What faith they had because you know the Amazon is full of things that can eat you.

We made glasses for the people; even the chief got a pair of them. Our eye doctor was from Alaska where you can see the northern lights. He had his whole family there. The doctors that came with us did minor medical procedures. There are no doctors' offices or hospitals for miles; transportation was only by boat. There aren't any roads, so there aren't any cars in the jungle. Now and then, a boat would come through for medical reasons or dental procedures.

We had great worship services, and because of the language (Portuguese), there was always an interpreter. Some of the missionaries were fluent in Portuguese. There were missionaries from Mozambique, Africa, Cambodia, Mongolia, Thailand, Alaska, and across the United States. This was the second mission's trip of *Far-Flung Tin Can*; I missed the first one. I had great conversations with the missionaries especially from Mongolia. I've always been fascinated with that part of the world.

The church of Brazil was so gracious in getting us where we needed to go. The overseer said, "The church of Brazil was in great need of prayer because witchcraft is always trying to get a foothold." We prayed nonstop in the villages during the services. We cast out demons and prayed for many to be healed.

The next stop would be the baptizing. During that time, I had got sick from I'm not sure, but the Lord gave me the scripture where God told Naaman to dip himself in the Jordan to be healed of leprosy. So I laid down everything that would get wet besides my clothes and got baptized in the Amazon River. In one hour, I was healed. It was a miracle.

I got a selfie with the main chief and a picture with the captain and his first mate. I told them I am retired Navy, so the first mate showed me the engine compartment (a powerful engine drove the small ship).

The captain took us to his home. It was a floating home (it was really cool); we moored right beside his house. We saw crocodiles and monkeys and a sloth. I held a baby croc. There were other strange animals that we could hear, but maybe it was best that we left them alone. I brought Brenda back a (stuffed) piranha, and she loved it.

At the end of our journey, we took a bus for a Brazilian steak dinner. Again, it was a long flight back home with lots of connecting flights. Far-Flung Tin Can recorded a number of spectacular songs up and down the Amazon. What a blessing it was to be with the group on this epic journey.

Next, I think they will be breaking ground to build a church (*where no man has gone before*). Check out *Far-Flung Tin Can* on Facebook, and get the DVD *Destination Amazon Together Chapter Two* and watch out for the tarantulas.

The picture on the cover was taken by the author off the coast of Cuba while serving with the US Navy.

Ted and his brothers and sisters grew up in church and went to a parochial school, which probably kept them out of trouble. Right after high school, Ted joined the Navy and went off to basic training. Ted met people from all over the country and backgrounds. They had religious services every Sunday in boot camp.

Later, he was introduced to other religions for a few years. After release from active service with the US Navy, he continued to stay in the naval reserve. A young preacher came in on Sundays, so the troops wouldn't miss Sunday service. His preaching and teaching were sound and had an effect on Ted. It took a few years, and finally, his heart cracked open; the truth in Jesus Christ was manifested, and he received Jesus Christ as his personal savior.

He went to different churches, seeking the truth. He enrolled in Bible college for a period of time and even wrote a book (*Breaking Thru*). This book (*The Depth of the Soul*), however, is a continuation of his studies and meditation on the Word and travels with the military and mission trips around the world. It is clear to Ted that the planet is in need of a savior and the truth that Jesus Christ brings especially the United States of America. Jesus is coming soon.